FLYING
is my favorite
F-word

a kick-ass collection
of aviation quotes

COPYRIGHT © 2025 BY JILL HOGAN

ALL RIGHTS RESERVED. NO PART OF THIS BOOK MAY BE REPRODUCED, STORED IN A RETRIEVAL SYSTEM, OR TRANSMITTED IN ANY FORM OR BY ANY MEANS— ELECTRONIC, MECHANICAL, PHOTOCOPYING, RECORDING, OR OTHERWISE—WITHOUT THE PRIOR WRITTEN PERMISSION OF THE AUTHOR.

DISCLAIMER:

THE QUOTES IN THIS BOOK ARE PRESENTED AS A COLLECTION OF PERSONAL INSIGHTS AND INSPIRATIONS, UNLESS OTHERWISE NOTED. WHILE EVERY EFFORT HAS BEEN MADE TO CREDIT SOURCES ACCURATELY, SOME ENTRIES MAY REFLECT GENERAL THEMES OR COMMON SAYINGS RATHER THAN SPECIFIC ATTRIBUTIONS. THIS COLLECTION IS INTENDED FOR MOTIVATIONAL AND INFORMATIONAL PURPOSES ONLY.

PRINTED AND BOUND IN THE UNITED STATES OF AMERICA

1ST EDITION

THIS IS NO ORDINARY QUOTE BOOK, SO FASTEN YOUR SEATBELT!

FLYING MY FAVORITE F-WORD
a kick-ass collection of aviation quotes

THIS BOOK IS FILLED WITH INSPIRATION, HUMOR, AND HONESTY ABOUT PILOTS AND THE LIFE THEY LIVE. WHEN YOU PICK UP THIS BOOK, YOU'RE GOING TO BE READING INSPIRING WORDS THAT WILL MOTIVATE, ENTERTAIN, AND MAKE YOU LAUGH, ALL AT A PILOT'S EXPENSE!

THIS IS THE IDEAL GIFT FOR AVIATION ENTHUSIASTS, THEIR LOVED ONES, THOSE WHO SUPPORT THEM, AND, OF COURSE, ALL PILOTS: COMMERCIAL PILOTS, CARGO PILOTS, CHARTER PILOTS, CORPORATE PILOTS, MILITARY PILOTS, HELICOPTER PILOTS, RICH GUY PILOTS, TEST PILOTS, BANNER-TOW PILOTS, BUSH PILOTS, SEAPLANE PILOTS, NARCO PILOTS, GLIDER PILOTS, AERIAL SURVEY PILOTS, AIR AMBULANCE PILOTS, STUDENT PILOTS, ADVENTURE-SEEKING PILOTS, FIREFIGHTING PILOTS, INFLUENCER PILOTS, SKYDIVING JUMP PILOTS, DRONE PILOTS, FLIGHT INSTRUCTOR PILOTS, SPACECRAFT PILOTS, SEARCH AND RESCUE PILOTS, SUPPORT PILOTS, STUNT PILOTS, CROP DUSTER PILOTS, HUMANITARIAN AID PILOTS, AND EVERY OTHER PILOT NOT LISTED BUT STILL FLYING HIGH.

TOP REASONS TO HAVE THIS BOOK:

- IT'S A GREAT WAY TO CONNECT WITH A PILOT
- IT GIVES A FEELING OF RELAXATION AND HAPPINESS WHEN STRESSED
- IT'S A GREAT AVIATION GIFT FOR THAT SPECIAL SOMEONE
- IT'S HIGHLY ENTERTAINING
- IT JUST BRINGS JOY TO THOSE WHO READ IT

PERFECT FOR GRADUATIONS, RETIREMENTS, BIRTHDAYS, OR JUST BECAUSE. THIS QUOTE BOOK IS FOR ANYONE WHO LOVES AVIATION.

Author's Note

This book is a collection of famous, inspirational, and humorous quotes gathered from years of being surrounded by the world of aviation. My love for aviation started early, I was eight years old and my dad's friend owned an airplane and gave my dad and me a ride. From that moment on, aviation has always been part of my world. I grew up going to airshows, watching my older brother work as an aircraft mechanic, and eventually saw my husband, a few nephews, friends, and my son become pilots. Aviation is the soundtrack of our home. From the dinner table to the living room, there's always some kind of pilot talk happening.

You'll notice not every quote in this book has a name or attribution. Some pages are timeless hangar talk with no known source, and others are things you hear over radios or stumble across while scrolling. I've credited everyone I could, and the rest are here because they capture the heart of flying in a way that's too good to leave out.

This book is also a bit of a family affair. A quote from Kyah and one from Zander, two of my incredibly sharp and hilarious kids, are included. Zander is a pilot with a sharp wit and a love for flying, while Kyah is a gifted writer with a no-nonsense perspective and a knack for calling things exactly as she sees them. The visual magic? That's thanks to my daughter, Chloe, a truly gifted artist whose creativity helped bring some of these pages to life.

And finally, the real inspiration behind this book: my husband, Rick. We met in high school, and he truly won my heart back when he was just a cute, nerdy boy with a kind heart and big dreams. I didn't choose him because he was going to be a pilot, but when I found out he was heading to college for aviation, I definitely thought that was pretty cool. He's one of the hardest working pilots I've ever known. His tireless dedication to making aviation safer, smarter, and better for every pilot out there is what keeps me dreaming, creating, and endlessly proud to be by his side. I've supported him and our family through every phase of our aviation life - from his training and long trips, to months overseas with no clear idea of when he'd be able to come home, to packing up our family and living all over the United States. None of it has ever been easy, but it's made us stronger. Aviation life isn't always simple, but I wouldn't trade it for anything.

Clear skies,

Jill Hogan

FLYING IS HYPNOTIC, AND ALL PILOTS ARE WILLING VICTIMS TO THE SPELL.

Ernest K. Gann

growing up optional

AVIATION IS SAID TO BE OVER A HUNDRED YEARS OLD WITH THOUSANDS OF MYSTERIES... OR MAYBE IT'S A THOUSAND YEARS OLD WITH HUNDREDS OF MYSTERIES. WELL, THAT IS JUST ONE OF THE MYSTERIES.

Rick Hogan

WELCOME TO AVIATION!

YOU ARE NOW BROKE

PILOTS TAKE NO SPECIAL JOY IN WALKING; THEY LIKE FLYING.

Neil Armstrong

THERE'S ONLY ONE JOB IN THIS WORLD THAT GIVES YOU AN OFFICE IN THE SKY, AND THAT IS A PILOT.

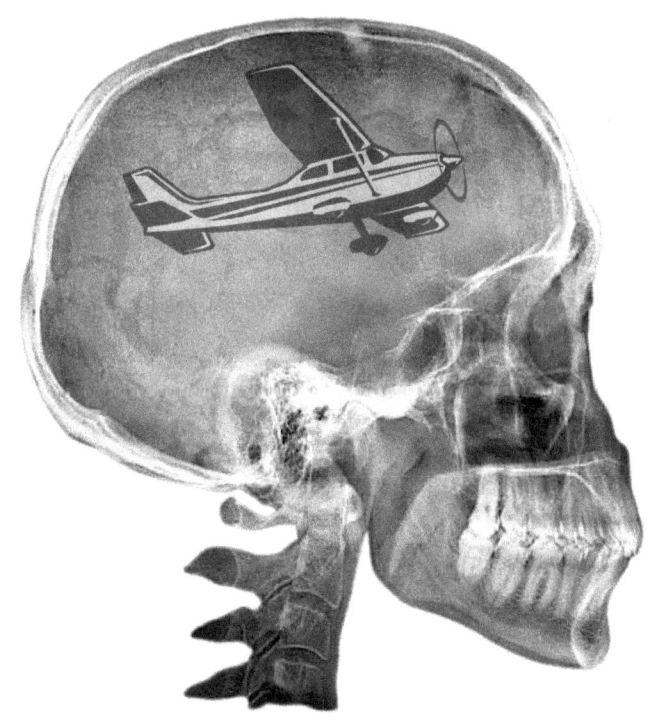

THE ENGINE IS THE HEART OF THE AIRPLANE, BUT THE PILOT IS ITS SOUL.

Sir Walter Alexander Raleigh

DO YOU
EVEN

LIFT
BRO?

WHEN EVERYTHING SEEMS TO BE GOING AGAINST YOU, REMEMBER THAT AN AIRPLANE TAKES OFF AGAINST THE WIND, NOT WITH IT.

Henry Ford

It's better to be on the ground wishing you were in the sky than in the sky wishing you were on the ground.

ALL MEN ARE CREATED EQUAL, BUT ONLY THE FINEST BECOME PILOTS

FLYING IS LEARNING HOW TO THROW YOURSELF AT THE GROUND AND MISS.

Douglas Adams

QUESTION:
HOW DO YOU KNOW IF THERE IS A PILOT IN THE ROOM?

ANSWER:
THEY WILL TELL YOU.

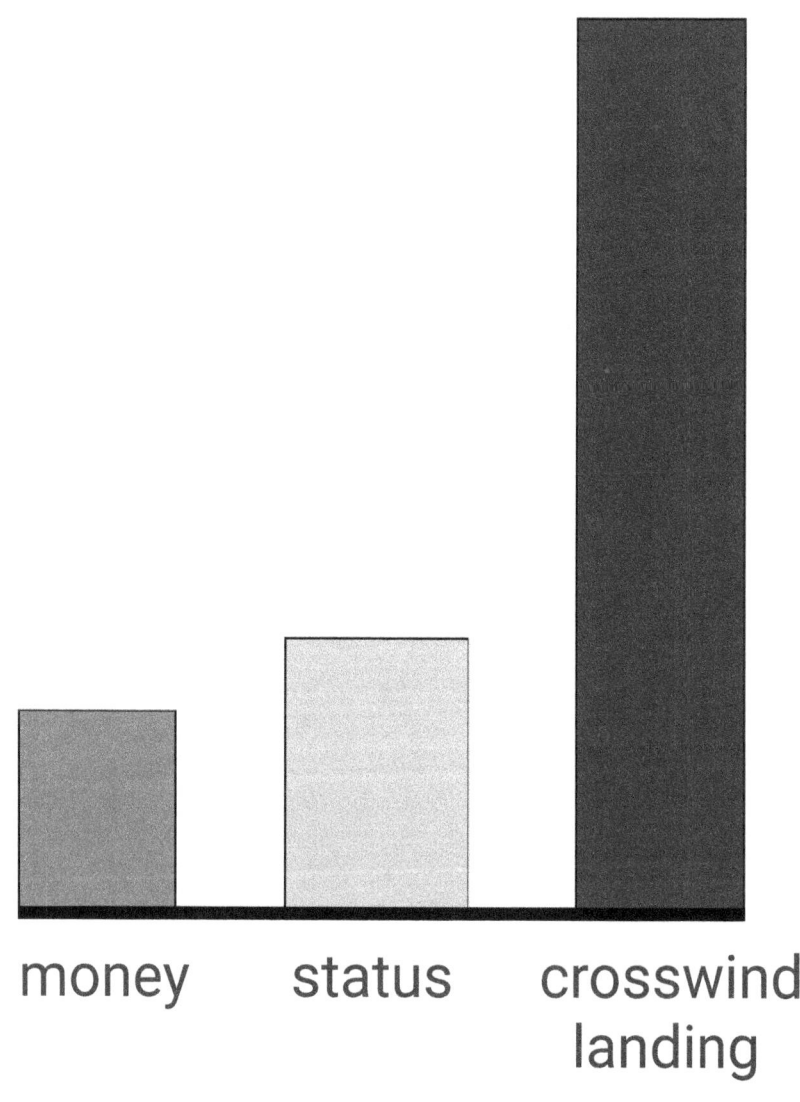

EVERY PILOT THINKS THEY'RE THE BEST PILOT IN THE WORLD. I THINK I'M THE BEST PILOT.

Gordon Bethune

WHY I WANT TO BE A PILOT

WRITTEN BY A 3RD GRADER

I want to be a pilot when I grow up because it's a fun job and easy to do. That's why there are so many pilots flying around today.

Pilots don't need much school, they just have to learn to read numbers so they can read instruments. I guess they should be able to read road maps so they can find their way if they get lost.

Pilots should be brave so they won't be scared if it's foggy and they can't see, or if a wing or motor falls off, they should stay calm. Pilots have to have good eyes to see through clouds, and they can't be afraid of lightning or thunder because they're closer to them than we are.

The salary pilots make is another thing I like. They make more money than they can spend. This is because most people think plane flying is dangerous, except pilots don't because they know how easy it is.

There isn't much I don't like, except that girls like pilots and all the stewardesses want to marry pilots, so they always have to chase them away so they won't bother them.

I hope I don't get airsick because I get carsick, and if I get airsick I couldn't be a pilot and then I'd have to go to work.

ONCE YOU HAVE TASTED FLIGHT, YOU WILL FOREVER WALK THE EARTH WITH YOUR EYES TURNED SKYWARD, FOR THERE YOU HAVE BEEN, AND THERE YOU WILL ALWAYS LONG TO RETURN.

Leonardo da Vinci

HE WHO WOULD LEARN TO FLY ONE DAY MUST FIRST LEARN TO STAND AND WALK AND RUN AND CLIMB AND DANCE; ONE CANNOT FLY INTO FLYING.

Friedrich Nietzsche

7 DAYS
WITHOUT FLYING

MAKES
1 WEAK

YOU HAVEN'T SEEN A TREE UNTIL YOU'VE SEEN ITS SHADOW FROM THE SKY.

Amelia Earhart

THERE'S NO SUCH THING AS A NATURAL-BORN PILOT.

Chuck Yeager

Test Results:

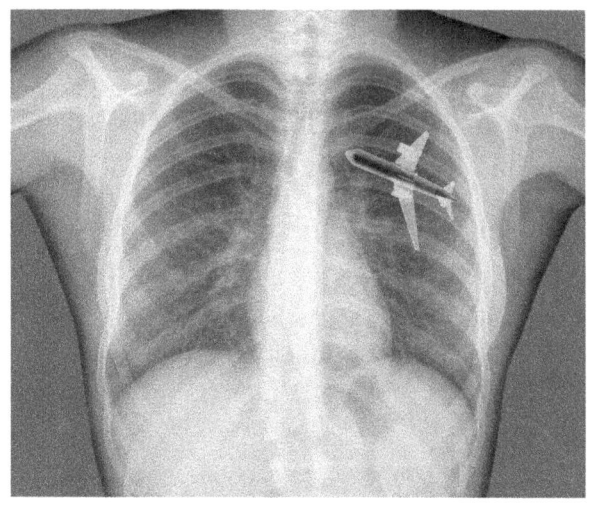

FINDINGS:
1. The cardiac silhouette appears unusually shaped, resembling the fuselage of an airplane.
2. The aorta curves like a wing, and the heart's chambers mimic the cockpit and engines.
3. No abnormal fluid accumulation observed, but a slight turbulence pattern in the lungs, suggesting high altitude dreams.
4. The heart's rhythm is consistent with steady takeoff and smooth landings, no signs of distress.

IMPRESSION:
The pilot's heart is structurally sound, but its flight path shows a strong desire to soar. Recommend flying as much as possible, keeping the wings level and the engines running smoothly.

PILOTS ARE DRAWN TO FLYING BECAUSE IT'S A PERFECT COMBINATION OF SCIENCE, ROMANCE, AND ADVENTURE.

Charles Lindbergh

GOOD PEOPLE DO EXIST

THEY ARE JUST BUILDING AIRPLANES, BUYING AIRPLANES, THINKING ABOUT BUYING AN AIRPLANE, BUYING PARTS TO FIX AIRPLANES, TALKING ABOUT AIRPLANES, FLYING AIRPLANES...

IF YOU WANT TO GROW OLD AS A PILOT, YOU'VE GOT TO KNOW WHEN TO PUSH IT AND WHEN TO BACK OFF.

Chuck Yeager

MILF

MAN I LOVE FLYING

TEACH YOUR CHILD THE LOVE OF FLYING, AND THEY WILL NEVER HAVE MONEY FOR DRUGS.

MORE RIGHT RUDDER

WHEN FLYING THROUGH THUNDERSTORMS, A PILOT MAY EARN HIS FULL PAY FOR THAT YEAR IN LESS THAN TWO MINUTES. AT THE TIME OF THE INCIDENT, HE WOULD GLADLY RETURN THE ENTIRE AMOUNT FOR THE PRIVILEGE OF BEING ELSEWHERE.

Ernest K. Gann

ALL HAIL

Boeing 747

Queen of the Skies

NEVER FIND YOURSELF SHORT OF ALTITUDE, AIRSPEED OR IDEAS.

PREPARE FOR THE UNKNOWN, UNEXPECTED, AND INCONCEIVABLE... AFTER 50 YEARS OF FLYING, I'M STILL LEARNING EVERY TIME I FLY.

Gene Cernan

I NEED A HUG_e

Airplane

A SUPERIOR PILOT USES HIS SUPERIOR JUDGMENT TO AVOID SITUATIONS WHICH REQUIRE THE USE OF HIS SUPERIOR SKILL.

Frank Borman

A SMOOTH SEA NEVER MADE A SKILLED SAILOR, JUST AS CALM SKIES NEVER MADE A SKILLED PILOT.

FLYING
is my favorite
f-word

FLYING IS THE SECOND GREATEST THRILL KNOWN TO MAN. LANDING IS THE FIRST.

Frank Borman

IT IS POSSIBLE TO FLY WITHOUT MOTORS, BUT NOT WITHOUT KNOWLEDGE AND SKILL.

Wilbur Wright

BORN to FLY

AVIATION IS PROOF THAT, GIVEN THE WILL, WE HAVE THE CAPACITY TO ACHIEVE THE IMPOSSIBLE.

Eddie Rickenbacker

EVERY DAY IS A GOOD DAY WHEN YOU FLY.

IF YOU'RE FACED WITH A FORCED LANDING, FLY THE THING AS FAR INTO THE CRASH AS POSSIBLE.

Bob Hoover

a mile of highway will take you just a mile

A MILE OF RUNWAY WILL TAKE YOU ANYWHERE

AVIATE
NAVIGATE
COMMUNICATE

THE AIR UP THERE IN THE CLOUDS IS VERY PURE AND FINE, BRACING AND DELICIOUS. AND WHY SHOULDN'T IT BE? IT IS THE SAME AIR THE ANGELS BREATHE.

Mark Twain

The way a pilot thinks

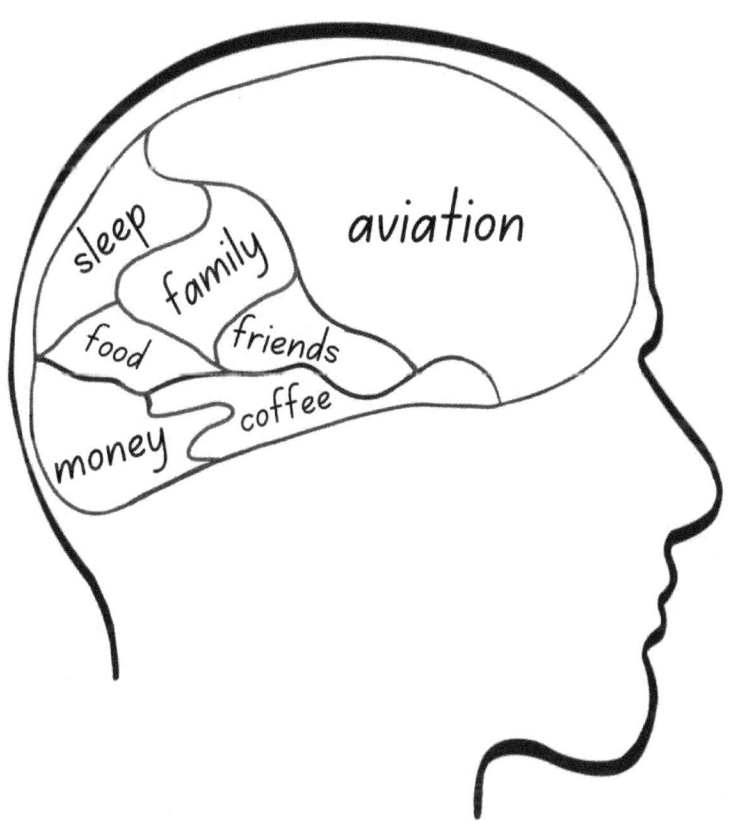

THERE IS NO SPORT EQUAL TO THAT WHICH AVIATORS ENJOY WHILE BEING CARRIED THROUGH THE AIR ON GREAT WHITE WINGS.

Wilbur Wright

THE FOUR FORCES OF FLIGHT

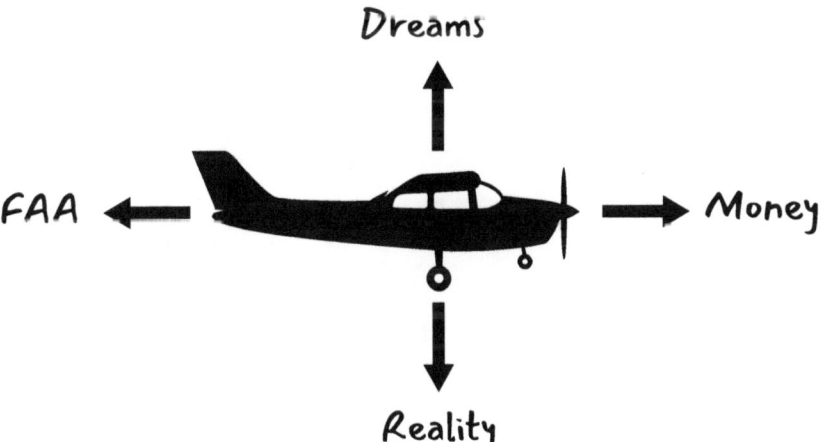

I CAN'T DEFINE THE MOMENT WHEN I SAID, "I'M GOING TO BE A PILOT." IT WAS JUST A FEELING OF ALWAYS WANTING TO BE FREE.

Jacqueline Cochran

PILOT FAITH

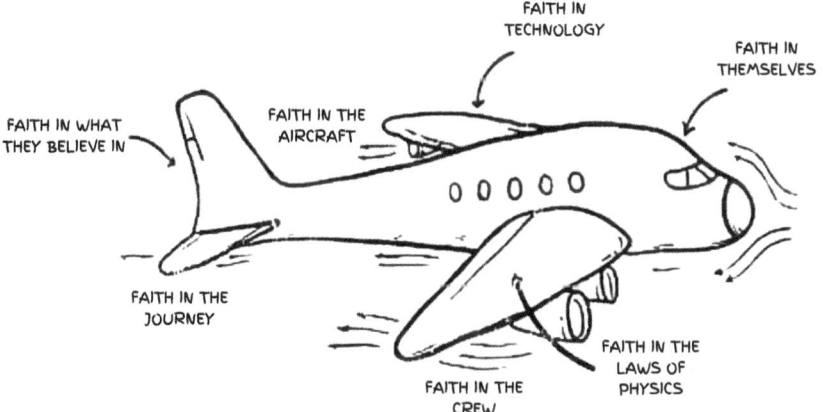

A PILOT LIVES IN A WORLD OF PERFECTION OR NOT AT ALL.

Jacqueline Cochran

GOING UP IS OPTIONAL,

COMING DOWN IS MANDATORY.

TO BE A PILOT IS TO LEARN HOW TO MANAGE FEAR AND HOW TO EMBRACE THE THRILL OF THE UNKNOWN.

Antoine de Saint-Exupéry

A PILOT WHO SAYS HE HAS NEVER BEEN FRIGHTENED IN AN AIRPLANE IS, I'M AFRAID, LYING.

Louise Thaden

I KNOW THERE'S MONEY IN AVIATION, I PUT IT THERE.

THE BEST PILOTS FLY MORE THAN THE OTHERS; THAT'S WHY THEY'RE THE BEST.

Chuck Yeager

THE MOST PROFOUND JOY IS FLYING. I FEEL LIKE I'VE ENTERED ANOTHER WORLD.

JFK Jr.

If you're dating a pilot, raise your glass; if you're not, elevate your standards.

GREAT PILOTS ARE MADE NOT BORN. . .
A MAN MAY POSSESS GOOD EYESIGHT, SENSITIVE HANDS, AND PERFECT COORDINATION, BUT THE END RESULT IS ONLY FASHIONED BY STEADY COACHING, MUCH PRACTICE, AND EXPERIENCE.

Johnnie Johnson

CHECK OUT MY

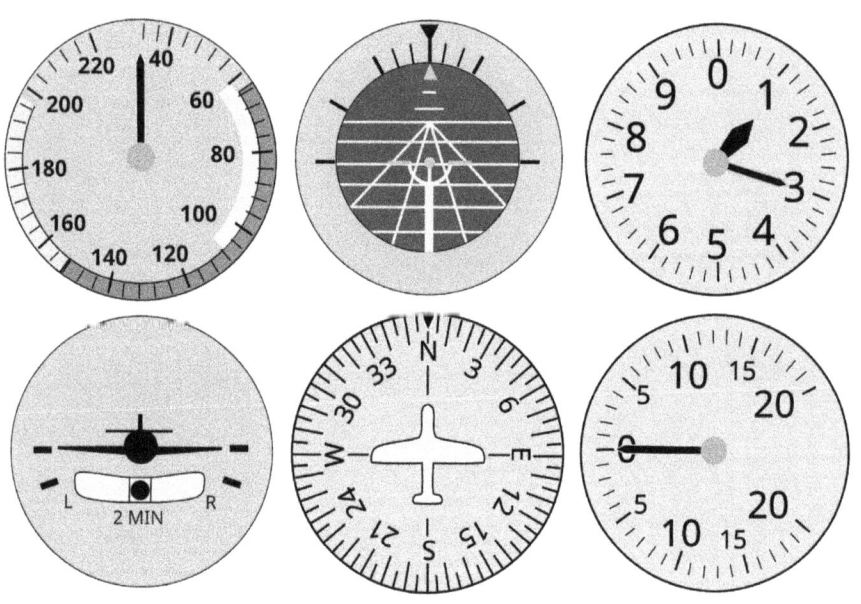

SIX PACK

DEATH IS THE HANDMAIDEN OF THE PILOT; SOMETIMES IT COMES BY ACCIDENT, SOMETIMES BY AN ACT OF GOD.

Scott Crossfield

Pilot Life Is

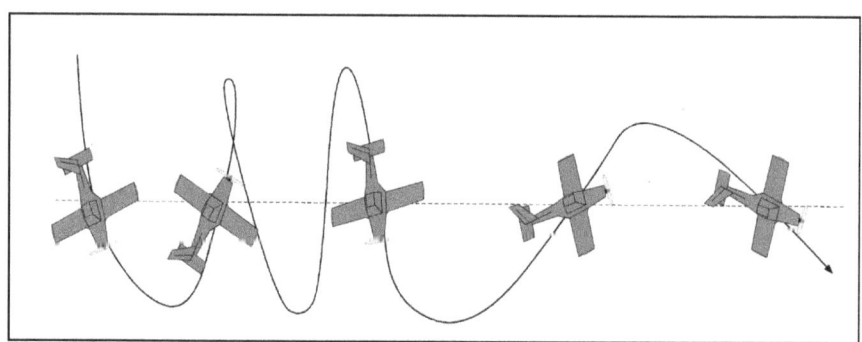

ALL ABOUT STABILITY

IF YOU ARE BORED FLYING, YOUR STANDARDS ARE TOO LOW.

Lauran Paine Jr.

The SKY is not the LIMIT

It's just the beginning

The freedom of owning an airplane is the ability to decide when you will go, where you will go, and how you will get there. Unless the weather is bad, then you may need to change your plans.

PILOTS
GETTING PAID
to get high

I CANNOT DESCRIBE THE DELIGHT, THE WONDER, AND THE INTOXICATION OF THIS FREE DIAGONAL MOVEMENT ONWARD AND UPWARD.

Alberto Santos-Dumont

I *am a* PILOT

I CAN'T FIX IDIOTS
BUT I CAN TAKE
THEM FAR AWAY

NO WISE PILOT, NO MATTER HOW GREAT HIS TALENT AND EXPERIENCE, FAILS TO USE HIS CHECKLIST.

Charlie Munger

TWO WRONGS DON'T MAKE A RIGHT

BUT TWO WRIGHTS MADE A PLANE

WHEN FLYING, THE ONLY TIME YOU HAVE TOO MUCH FUEL IS WHEN YOU'RE ON FIRE

Ernest K. Gann

PILOTS:

LOOKING DOWN ON PEOPLE SINCE 1903

AS FLYING ENTERS INTO EVERYDAY LIFE, THE DREAMS OF CENTURIES BECOME ACTUALITIES. ONE BY ONE THEY TAKE SHAPE AND BECOME STEPPING-STONES FOR OTHER DREAMS.

Amelia Earhart

I HATE BEING SEXY

BUT I AM A PILOT
SO I CAN'T HELP IT

FLYING WITHOUT FEATHERS IS NOT EASY; MY WINGS HAVE NO FEATHERS.

Plautus

I'm not an angel

but i can still fly

I LOVE FLYING PLANES AND RIDING BIKES. THAT'S WHY I'VE GOT EIGHT OF EACH OF THEM (OR IS IT NINE?)

Harrison Ford

SLEEPING POSITIONS

Architect

Teacher

Engineer

Pilot

I HAVE LOVED AVIATION FOR ALL MY LIFE. THERE IS NO FEELING IN THE WORLD QUITE LIKE FLYING AN AIRPLANE.

John Travolta

This is how a pilot rolls

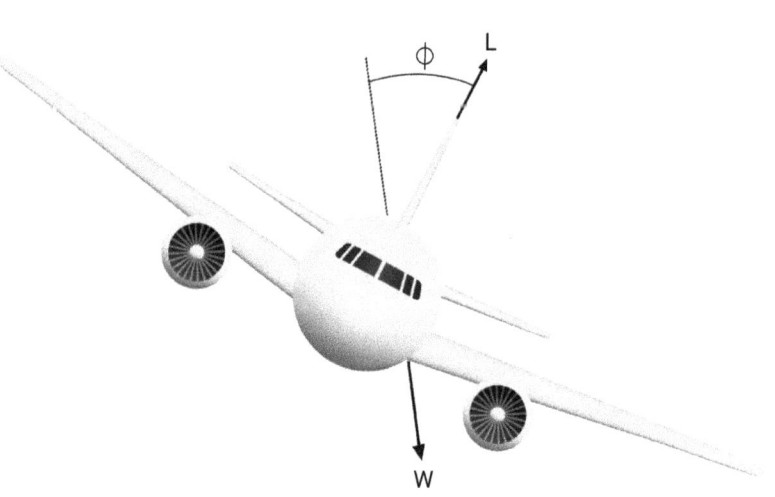

FLYING HAS ALWAYS BEEN ONE OF MY GREATEST PASSIONS. IT GIVES ME A SENSE OF FREEDOM AND EXHILARATION.

JFK Jr.

QUESTION:
HOW DO YOU MAKE A SMALL FORTUNE IN AVIATION?

ANSWER:
START WITH A LARGE FORTUNE.

THE GREATER THE DIFFICULTY, THE MORE GLORY IN SURMOUNTING IT. SKILLFUL PILOTS GAIN THEIR REPUTATION FROM STORMS AND TEMPESTS.

Epictetus

How a pilot's heart beats

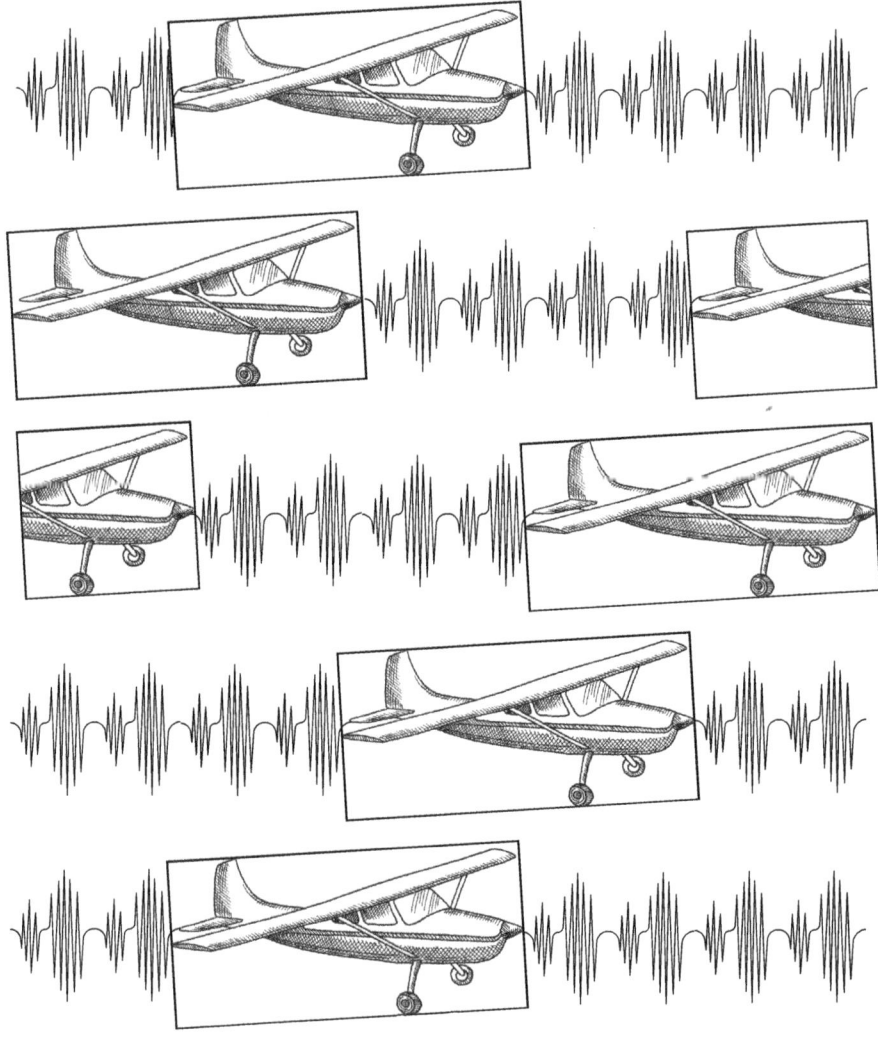

PILOTS ARE A RARE KIND OF HUMAN. THEY LEAVE THE ORDINARY SURFACE OF THE WORLD TO PURIFY THEIR SOUL IN THE SKY, AND THEY COME DOWN TO EARTH ONLY AFTER RECEIVING THE COMMUNION OF THE INFINITE.

Jose Maria Velasco Ibarra

THERE WAS A TIME WHEN I NEEDED TO SIT ON A CUSHION TO SEE OUT THE FRONT WINDOW OF A CESSNA 152. BUT I LEARNED THAT GROWING UP TO BE A PILOT WASN'T JUST ABOUT GETTING TALLER; IT WAS ABOUT GROWING IN CONFIDENCE, PERSEVERANCE, AND PASSION.

Claire Lemiski

sometimes the smallest airplanes give us the **BIGGEST DREAMS**

MOST GULLS DON'T BOTHER TO LEARN MORE THAN THE SIMPLEST FACTS OF FLIGHT — HOW TO GET FROM SHORE TO FOOD AND BACK AGAIN. FOR MOST GULLS, IT IS NOT FLYING THAT MATTERS, BUT EATING. FOR THIS GULL, THOUGH, IT WAS NOT EATING THAT MATTERED, BUT FLIGHT.

Jonathan Livingston Seagull

Rule #1
THE PILOT IS ALWAYS RIGHT

Rule #2
IF THE PILOT IS WRONG, REFER TO RULE #1

MY SOUL IS IN THE SKY.

William Shakespeare

NOTHING IS CERTAIN IN LIFE BUT DEATH, TAXES, AND A PILOT LETTING YOU KNOW HE'S A PILOT.

Any landing you can walk away from is a good one. A great landing is one where you can use the plane again.

FLYING IS HYPNOTIC, AND ALL YOU DO IS STEP INTO THE PLANE, AND AFTER THAT, IT DOES ALL THE WORK.

Jimmy Buffett

I HATE WHEN PEOPLE FIND OUT THAT

I'M A PILOT

AVIATION MATH

OF TAKEOFFS = # OF LANDINGS

TO DESCRIBE THE THRILL OF FLYING TO SOMEONE WHO HAS NEVER FLOWN IS LIKE TRYING TO EXPLAIN MUSIC TO SOMEONE WHO HAS NEVER HEARD IT.

Jimmy Buffett

AVIATION HAS ALWAYS BEEN A PART OF MY LIFE. MY DAD WAS AN AVIATOR, AND I HAD THE CHANCE TO GROW UP AROUND PLANES, SO I KNEW I WANTED TO BE A PILOT.

John Travolta

THINGS PILOTS DO IN THEIR SPARE TIME.

GO FLYING

WATCH PLANES

RESEARCH PLANES

TALK ABOUT FLYING

THINK ABOUT FLYING

DREAM ABOUT FLYING

THE BEST THING ABOUT FLYING IS BEING UP THERE ON YOUR OWN. YOU'RE PART OF THE SKY, AND THE PLANE JUST FEELS LIKE AN EXTENSION OF YOUR BODY.

Harrison Ford

PILOT:

A highly skilled person who expertly pushes buttons, speaks fluent radio code, and performs calculated guesswork, all while mastering the sky.

- *See also wizard, magician*

Not to be confused with:

- ✈ **A pirate** - both wear cool hats, love adventure, and talk in code.
- ✈ **A riot** - what happens when the in-flight snacks run out.
- ✈ **Quiet** - the sound of the pilot after flying for weeks.

MAN, I FREAKING LOVE FLYING!

Zander Hogan

FLYING IS LIKE GOOD MUSIC: IT ELEVATES THE SPIRIT, AND IT'S AN EXHILARATING FREEDOM.

Harrison Ford

LANDING SAFELY

THE MOST IMPORTANT PART OF FLYING

THERE ARE OLD PILOTS AND THERE ARE BOLD PILOTS, BUT THERE ARE NO OLD BOLD PILOTS

E. Hamilton Lee

Before Pilot's license   After Pilot's license

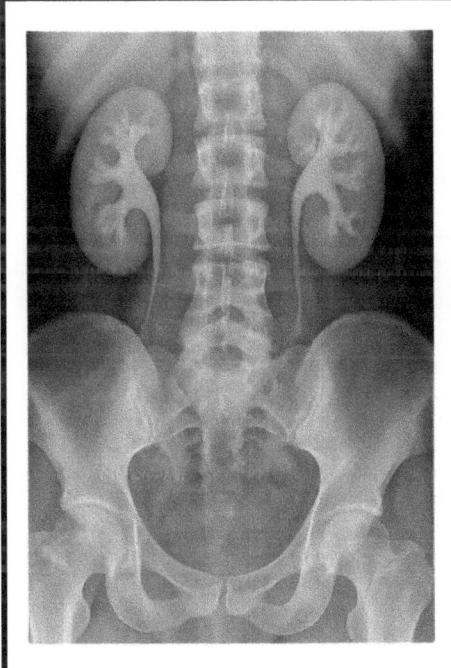 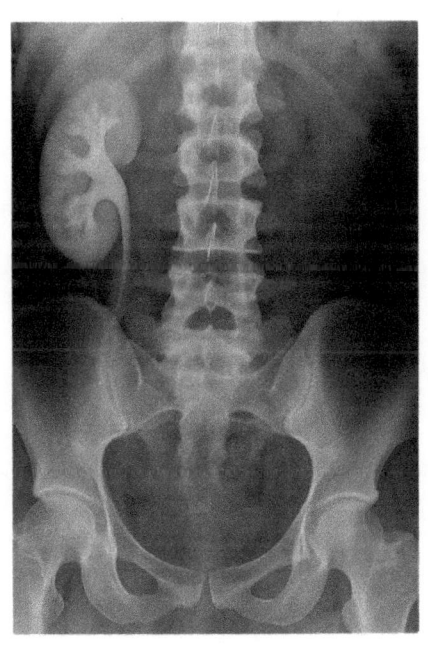

TO BE A PILOT IS TO EMBODY THE SPIRIT OF SPEED, PRECISION, AND FEARLESSNESS.

THERE'S MORE TO LIFE THAN BEING A PASSENGER.

Amelia Earhart

IN MORE THAN 120 YEARS OF FLYING

WE HAVE YET TO LEAVE ONE UP THERE

FLYING IS SOMETHING THAT I'VE ALWAYS WANTED TO DO. AS A KID, IT WAS ABOUT ADVENTURE AND EXPLORATION.

Tom Cruise

FLYING IS A VERY CONTROLLED AND DISCIPLINED ENVIRONMENT. IT'S NOT SOMETHING YOU DO LIGHTLY.

Gary Numan

WHEN I'M UP IN THE AIR, EVERYTHING ELSE DISAPPEARS. IT'S JUST ME AND THE SKY.

Gary Numan

ALWAYS BE YOURSELF

unless you can be a pilot

THEN ALWAYS BE A PILOT

QUESTION:
WHAT IS THE PRIMARY USE OF THE PROPELLER?

ANSWER:
TO COOL THE PILOT. WHEN THE PROPELLER STOPS SPINNING, THE PILOT STARTS SWEATING.

THERE IS FREEDOM WAITING FOR YOU ON THE BREEZES OF THE SKY. AND YOU ASK, "WHAT IF I FALL?" OH, BUT MY DARLING, WHAT IF YOU FLY?

Erin Hanson

If you aren't happy single, you won't be happy married. Happiness comes from airplanes, it doesn't come from relationships.

AND LET'S GET ONE THING STRAIGHT. THERE'S A BIG DIFFERENCE BETWEEN A PILOT AND AN AVIATOR. ONE IS A TECHNICIAN; THE OTHER IS AN ARTIST IN LOVE WITH FLIGHT.

E. B. Jeppesen

AVIATION IN ITSELF IS NOT INHERENTLY DANGEROUS. BUT TO AN EVEN GREATER DEGREE THAN THE SEA, IT IS TERRIBLY UNFORGIVING OF ANY CARELESSNESS, INCAPACITY, OR NEGLECT.

Ernest K. Gann

ALTITUDE
AIRSPEED
BRAINS

  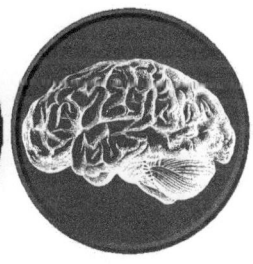

Two are always needed to successfully complete a flight

Money does not BUY HAPPINESS

BUT IT DOES BUY FLYING LESSONS

Which is pretty much the same thing

A PILOT HAS NO SHORTAGE OF PHRASES ABOUT HOW AMAZING HE IS. JUST ASK HIM AND HE WILL TELL YOU TWICE.

Kyah Hogan

www.ingramcontent.com/pod-product-compliance
Lightning Source LLC
Chambersburg PA
CBHW050734010526
44107CB00010B/843